Bury My Defiance

Whitnee Russell

ISBN-10: 0692185275
ISBN-13: 978-0692185278

DEDICATION

I dedicate this book to my beautiful daughter Ellis Ann. I pray you know your worth at every moment of the day. You can do nothing to drive my love away.

ACKNOWLEDGMENTS

To my sweet husband Cody, thank you for all the moments you stopped to listen to each word I've laid on your ears. The way you gently have taken care of my tears. The prayers, support and selflessness are beyond what my crazy dreams could believe I would have seen.

To my Mom, without you I would not be here. It's true. You gave your body for my expense but also countless heart stops, and crumbling within. You have been more than guidance but a friend to me. Thank you for your bravery.

To my Dad, Eddie, the one who stood there and chose. You took a broken family and helped make us whole.

To my Prayer warriors a tribute to all of you. You went before our King when I was weak and sometimes just did not want to. Thank you for all the prayers. I've needed each and every one of you. Thank you Lord for giving me so many people who care.

Eggshells

A smile and a wink.
Charming, classy people love you, they think.
Behind closed doors.
Anger steams from your pores.
Balancing on eggshells by age three.
Fathers shouldn't be this scary.
I learned of Heaven above.
I couldn't understand that type of love.
Terror stricken to think.
God's love must be a mistake.
If my earthy Father is like this.
Pass me by Jesus, I can resist.
This foxhole is quite nice.
Leave me alone.
I don't need someone else who just plays nice.

The Game

Addicted to a game I was taught as a kid, not knowing the
darkness it hid.
From the hands of someone filled with spite.
It plunders my soul but fills me with curious delight.
The game ravaged me with delirious shame,
at this point I'm the only one to blame.
Jesus, there is a canyon growing between you and I.
Reach out your hand.
I want to see you eye to eye.
Through all of this you have never left.
The grace you give is endless.
Take this thorn I give it to you.
I believe with you Abba, I am new.
Sanctified, whole, clean, and pure.
Lord, I lay down this affliction for you to endure.
I am free now, this I am sure.

The Porch

Getting my nerve pacing on the porch.
I see your truck flame down the street in a torch.
The knot grows the size of a boulder inside of me,
as I tell you how it's going to be.
You scare me, I hate you, leave this town.
All you have done is let me down.
I'm merely a child only the age of eight.
The heaviness a ten ton weight.
Jesus, how can a father treat a child like this?
It makes me not even want to call on you, my Savior in
distress.
The valley this created has worn me so thin.
Yet, I long to be close to you Savior, my friend.
I need a father to love me so true.
Please teach me that it's safe to let me love you.

Like the Lamb

You picked out my name.
Held me close even in physical pain.
Through every cry you were always there.
Kissing my hand to show me you care.
Though broken inside You held me to your chest.
Mom, You did your best.
Everything I know is because of you.
The sacrifice you gave is that of the Lamb.
Because you were broken in two.
You carry guilt for things I don't see.
You are brave, strong, loyal and full of generosity.
Without you,
I could be none of these things.
Mom, thank you for enduring like the Lamb.

Grafted In

Fathers are mean and scary.
That's all I knew until in walks you.
Choosing to take me on and make me a home.
A daddy to me,
That's how it will be.
Grafted in from today.
God's hand always at play.
Finally a daddy who will stay.

Love's Plan

Who am I to call you my father, to even be given a name.
Broken and hiding scared of deciding inside clinging to my
pain.
You see right through me, decide to pursue me and take on
all of this shame.
Father here I am, Jesus here I am.
Take me in your arms right now and love me only as you
can.
Blameless and hurting never deserting.
Sacrificial Lamb.
You saw right through me and called out to me and said
child, you are my plan.
Father here I am, Jesus here I am.
Take me in your arms right now and love me only as you
can.

Camp Yeshua

I count the stars feeling small in the dark.
Longing for love but not knowing where to start.
I feel your grace and gently understand that no other love
would die for fallen man.
Yeshua, Yeshua breathe life into me.
Yeshua, Yeshua pour love through me.
You paid the price to make the way.
Defeated the grave and rolled that stone away.
Yeshua, Yeshua shine light into me.
Yeshua, Yeshua burn bright through me.
In your hands you hold the stars.
Blazing through each one of your scars.
Yeshua, Yeshua.
I feel your grace and gently understand that no other love
would die for fallen man.

Songs in my Head

Singing a song in my head as I would lay as a child in my
bed.
It would tumble endlessly.
Words flowing tenderly.
My King.
I knew you in an intimate way.
Bouncing rhythm never astray.
Humming and praying out loud.
The joy I felt knowing you were around.
The innocent faith on those hot summer nights.
Mesmerized by bugs that sparkle with light.
Crickets helped me keep time and pace.
Lord, help me go back and remember that grace.

Builder

Broken standing alone falling apart to spaces I've lost to the dark.

Endless doubt not ready to part.

Feeling like home.

Lord see in me, Shine in me.

The places I've hidden away reconstruct how I've found my escape.

Reclaim what you've made and make me a home.

Designer, Builder, Creator.

I'm never alone you've made me a home.

Designed just for me how I'd love it to be.

I'm never alone you've made me a home.

A mansion on a hill.

Every room filled with your light.

The truth always in sight.

Redemption covers the walls your voice echoes the halls.

I'm never alone you've made me a home.

Blurred Edges

Three down.
Another on hand.
Blurring out images that fill me with dread.
Another.
Maybe two.
Lines are getting crossed.
Edges becoming askew.
Morning light.
Shines bright on the guilt from the night.
Soul crushing distance formed by my design.
Jesus you want to deliver, save and retrieve.
I'm going to grab another and find my own reprieve.

Tornado

Tough, not easy to crack.
I can handle my own and fire words right back.
No tear on this face.
I'll limp to the line then win the race.
Inside I'm so confused, a tornado of destruction.
A corrupt place of constant interruption.
My spirit a gaping tear.
I'm desperate for Yeshua to end this despair.
Come in.
Stop this at once.
I need you to take this punch.
I'm weak in need of the Redeemer you are.
I see your wounds and you bear all my scars.
I don't have to put on a show.
In you Christ Jesus my identity grows.
More of you less of me.
That's how I want my life to be.
I don't have to be tough or handle my own.
You paid the price on the cross alone.

The Road

Amazing grace never seemed sufficient to me.
A wretch never less, but I brought suffering.
Leading them down a hill with a cliff attached.
If they cried for help I turned my back.
Lord, I knew you but chose myself instead.
Please forgive me and the life I lead.
I give you my heart, Jesus.
It's yours to seize.
Help the people for the road I took them down.
Selfishly guided them to waters left to drown.
Mend each and every one.
Letting them know the full love of the Son.

Heart on the Run

I place my identity in a new start.
Pushing back deserving every part.
I will make my life right this time.
No help from anyone.
I was treated bad.
Don't I deserve a bit of fun?
Truth be told my heart is on the run.
From all the things I have done.
I feel I can't face the one who calls me Beloved.
Who took my place and shed his own blood.
Jesus shine your light in my fractured soul.
See where it needs mending and make it whole.
The fun I sought was empty brought shame and despair.
The only place I'm running is into your care.
Heal the people I hurt along the way.
My heart aches for them today.
Turn my distraction to beauty in their life.
Let them know my identity is made new when you paid the price.

Recurring Trap

My mind races to the worst possible scene.
Images dance around tumbling to a ravine.
Constantly wearing dark chains like a wrap.
Encompassing my thoughts like a recurring trap.
Leads me down a rabbit hole anxiety grips me again.
Darkness and shadows are where I begin.
This is too much to take.
Terror is echoing inside.
Causing every piece of me to quake.
Deliverer, I can't even whisper your name.
Search my soul.
Shine light even for a small piece to gain.
Take control I'm tired of sinking in the abyss.
Deliver me I beg you, Jesus.

Scar I Wear

Come to me.
I can't move.
I need you.
I'm broken, hungry, tired from my shame.
Lord, come to me.
All I can do is call out your name.
Jesus every scar I wear is causing me to tear.
Lord, come to me.
I can't even dare.
All I can do is whisper and hope my voice reaches your space.
Savior I give my all and fall to my face.
Pleading with every breath.
All I need Jehovah is rest.
Come to me.
I can't move.
I need you.

Patiently

Patiently waiting.
I don't deserve, all the knocks I have heard.
Lord your tenderness is present no matter how I turn.
Now that I've hit my knees closeness to you I yearn.
My tear stained face staring back at me.
Resembles nothing of how I use to be.
Savior, you graciously gave me a cure.
Holding tight, secure.
Knock and the door was open to me.
Sweet relief.
My Jesus.
There you stood.
Patiently.

Constant Friend

Fear my companion a steady constant friend.
I chose it to be my partner to defend.
Ransacked, tormented, deep aches.
Yet nurturing the open wound it makes.
Letting life pass stagnant from the toll.
Savior.
Heal these spots and the plague on my soul.
Anguish a playmate knocking at the door.
The familiar sound I've heard before.
How long will I play the victim in all of this?
Jesus, give me strength I need the rest.
Make me a Warrior kill fear today.
You said you would take all my burdens away.
Help me believe.
Lord this is true.
I am a Warrior.
Handing my fear to you.

Tapestry

Falling apart at the seams.
This world to the depth can be so mean.
Every part of the day I'm one thread away from unraveling.
I want to be woven into a tapestry of love.
Crafted through your blood.
Stitched together and complete.
Christ workmanship felt in each heartbeat.
A beautiful hand design.
To fulfill his purposeful outline.
Weave through me your tapestry.

Armor of Light

Worry and anxiety an ongoing plight.
I grow weary of the constant fight.
Gripped with fear stone by stone I build a wall.
Safe and sound in my town of
Jericho.
Lord, shout cause my terror to crumble and fall.
My red rope is a beacon for you to see,
you are my hope for bravery.
I give it all to you.
Cast the idols down let them turn to rumble too.
I have nothing to fear when you are near.
Perfect love cast out all the doubt, it disappears.
The Lord my God, Shout! Rejoice when the wall falls down.
I will be kneeling with my crown.
Ready to battle without any anxiety or fear.
A heart of courage for you are near.
It thumps day and night to the beat Adonai, Warrior, Lion,
let's fight.
Give me the armor of light.
Like a rock I stand,
never again on sinking sand.

Blinded no More

The world has doused the flame that was burning bright.
Light easily turns to night.
Eyes blinded stumbling, crawling from the fall.
Hosanna, have I grown so blind to it all?
To recognize you reaching out to me.
Lord I will sit still.
Patiently waiting for darkness to take a bow.
I can sense you now.
Peace.
Shining light when none was to be found.
Hope declaring a mighty sound.
The blessing in you is more than an offering.
A beacon of glory in you I will always be honoring.

Author of My Heart

I started this chapter on my own.
Aimless, my heart prone to roam.
Creating a story out of the dust.
Needing my Savior to reclaim what was lost.
Rewrite my story, let our romance progress. I am your bride
no blemish exists, clothed in fine linen waiting for you.
Authoring our love, Jesus, making my old story new.
I've relinquished to your point of view.
Savior, you will make this story end with a bountiful delight.
Every new chapter dripping with abundant grace. Salvation
from the master of my life. Dreaming of gazing at your face.
My story is not through. But in the end, I know the main point
was to honor you.

Battle Beloved

Take this vow my hand in yours.
Ups and downs both longing to be each other's cure.
Our thoughts not always pure.
Sleepless nights on the couch,
our minds spinning with doubt.
Blaming the other for things withheld.
First, we must die to self.
Jesus, place my resentment on the shelf.
Lord, we plead let us mimic you.
Love fully we are created to be one.
A mirror reflecting every hue.
Bless us in all of this.
We were once two, but we want one to exists.
Help our hearts fall genuinely in love with you, Emmanuel.
Now we have hope to persist and give you room to dwell.
Let us love one another as you have loved us first.
Grow through the years making past hurts disperse.
Love keeps no record of wrongs.
Lord, bind us together
make us strong.

We Fight

Pacing the room my knuckles white.
This rage inside I cannot fight.
I know you're lying again.
Hiding, and stabbing me in the back.
Love falling off track.
Suddenly your knees start to shake.
Your heart like alabaster, it crumbles.
You break.
Finally my husband I see you a man.
In need of forgiveness, love a friend.
I'm hurting, deeply, Lord I give this to you.
This brings up old wounds he swore he would not bruise.
Jesus, take this pain.
Let this be all for your gain.
Help us love one another through your heart not our sin.
Father, we are wounded but we want to win.
We are standing here together ready to endure this life.
Hand in hand for our marriage.
We Fight!

Write my Name

Is my heart like the Pharisee?
Throwing judgment down, wagging my finger for people to
see.
Shaking my head.
You deserve to be on the ground, shame only to be found.
Is my heart like the Pharisee when you come to me again?
Head hung in shame, needing a friend.
I see I am the Pharisee.
Treating you so wrong.
I've seen only your sin and in me I've done no harm.
Jesus, kneel and write my name.
Teach me to care not casting any blame.
I want the world to see.
I want to be taught by you and not a Pharisee.

Two Blue Lines

Two blue lines how can it be?
A miracle is growing inside of me.
My heart begins to race, as my mind tries to design your
sweet face.
Butterflies flicker creating a stir.
Dashing around life becoming a blur.
That's you I can feel.
Moments sinking in becoming real.
You are perfect it is true.
Our Creator himself designed you.
In my arms I finally understand.
The kind of love that loves like no other can.
My life I would give in your place.
You are my gift.
In you I see God's grace.

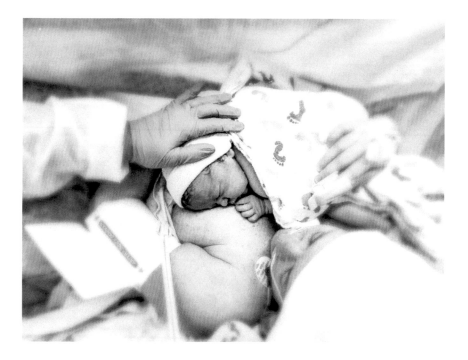

Mirror of Me

I hear you giggle in the other room.
Your laughter bursts like a balloon.
Marker highlights the wall.
I thank God for it all.
Every cry.
Every shout.
Even when I'm drowning in doubt.
My child you are my heart on a string.
You are my shadow a mirror of me.
Lord please open my eyes.
Let me see all you supply.
This beautiful gift entrusted to me.
Fills my soul with such glee.
How can I be worthy of you?
Jesus, you must see me blameless it's true.
To give something as precious as you.

Knight

You take her in your arms.
Spin her.
Feet never touching the ground.
She is your princess.
Never even having to wear a crown.
Daddy dance with me, is all she has to say.
You drop everything and whisk her away.
My love grows deeper as time goes on.
I see you as a Knight.
Letting the love of Christ shine bright.
Giving our daughter a safe home.
She will always be your princess.
It's so beautiful to me.
How God heals through you dancing our daughter with glee.

More Than I Deserve

Heels dug in I think I must win. Never will I give in.
I keep pushing designing my own life.
Creating deep caverns of strife.
If someone is in my way, I will not cave.
Callused by the street I've paved.
Jesus, I want to surrender my shattered plans.
That once were set in stone unmovable by man.
How can you love a heart so cold?
Grace flows from you with abundant force.
I see the mystery of you start to unfold.
Laying everything in your hands, my soul for you to hold.
Sweetly, you mend and preserve.
Then lavish me with more than I deserve.
Father, I give in. With you is where I win.
When my heels are dug in.

Chord of Three

Our love deepens richly with every season.
Through the darkest times we have sought the reason.
Intertwined to say the least.
An intricate design piece by piece.
As we lay our selfish ways aside.
To see each other and decide.
Our love for God holds us together.
Our faithfulness a tether.
Devotes us to the what may come.
Remembering the crucified son.
Saying I love you is so trite.
When the unity is beyond just you and I.
We are a chord of three.
God, you and me.

Make Time

Light turns to dark over and over stop and start.
The pace quickens everything's a blur.
Constant movements, the world you prefer.
Spend time with me, I'm only asking for a small part of your
day.
I want to know you in an intimate way.
Draw near to me.
Each wound I gladly took for your name.
I beat death to conquer your shame.
Make time for me, it's you I long to gain.
Just call out my name.
Yeshua, Messiah, Faithful and True.
Yeshua, Messiah, Faithful and True.
I will always make time for you.
Just call out my name.
Yeshua , Messiah, Faithful and True.
I will always make time for you.

Carved Out

Wooden edges frame my splintered heart.
Doubt and silence alone in the dark.
Memories of past regrets, things I didn't choose.
Reminding me how deeply I needed you.
I want to be Carved Out, guided to your door.
I want to be Carved Out, made just like before.
Every fiber a reconstructed view.
Reminding me how deeply I needed you.
You know me, You made me deep within my veins.
You see me, You love me,
You call me by my name.
Carved Out, love me just the same.
Carved Out, calling me by my name.
You are the carpenter I am the oak.
Carved Out, you bear my yoke.
Repurposed, polished, and designed to follow You.

Branded in Each Gash

God of Israel.
Death has no sting.
You conquered all for my suffering.
Taking every lash.
My name branded in each gash.
Jesus, you wear my filth so I am clean.
Even though you are my King.
I'm a peasant who spits in your face.
You shed your blood to show insatiable grace.
From now on I know where I stand.
Forever in the palm of your hand.

Bury my Defiance

Could I lay down with the lions?
Speak truth to the dyin'?
Sit alone in the silence and bury my defiance?
Not without you Lord, never without you.
Would I walk on stormy waters?
Turn my cheek to the scoffers?
Die for the deserting and forgive when I am hurting?
Not without you Lord, never without you.
Purposeful, Mighty, Holy and True.
You make me brave, Jehovah. I stand in awe of you.
NOW!
I can stand with the lions.
Speak truth to the dyin.'
Sit alone in the silence and bury my defiance.
I will brave stormy waters.
Turn my cheek to the scoffers.
Die for the deserting and forgive when I am hurting.
All because of you Lord, only because of You.

Engulf Me Lord

Alone at night planning ahead.
Counting out the day and the what said.
Missing the mark and just talking the talk.
My nature fears to let go of the walls I've built in the dark.
I split you up to fit you in my space, but the whole of you is
what I long to embrace.
Engulf me Lord.
Overwhelm my spirit take control.
Immerse me Lord, flood my soul.
Guard my heart, make me whole.
Make my nature bold.
Every wall made to dust, so I can pursue you with full trust.
Engulf me Lord.
Wash my mind, to be clean.
Baptized in you, whole and serene.

Key to my Soul

Breathe in me.
Fill me with what you believe.
I don't need all this world has to give.
Lord make me live.
You are the answer.
You are the key to my soul.
I give you all my thoughts.
Jesus, make me whole.
Shout in me!
Let me hear all that you say.
Hang on every command and pray.
You are the answer.
You are the key to my soul.
I give you all my thoughts.
Jesus, make me whole.
Breathe in me.
Shout in me!
You are the answer.
You are the key to my soul.

Sunday Best

Ruffled socks, shiny shoes, perfect smile inside so bruised.
Parted hair, pleats in place, walking tall wouldn't dare show
my true face.
Hi there, how are you, hurry up find my pew.
Sing the songs filled with hope fight the lump inside my
throat.
I feel you whisper softly to me, saying this isn't how it has to
be.
I made you for more than this.
You don't have to be your Sunday best.
I love you when you're a mess.
Unleash your soul and let it dance.
Scuffed up, burned out, giving my all.
Savior, I will praise you letting every burden fall.
You gave me a chance, now for you Jesus, I will dance.

Instrument

Like an instrument, ready to play.
Note by note, deeply it weighs.
Keeping time, on all my many wrongs.
Desperately, how my heart longs.
Beat by beat, to play a different tune.
The one that leads me back to you.
Savior, make me an instrument ready to play.
Making music, only for your praise.
Conduct me, and show me your ways.
Beat by beat, always for your praise.

Reserved No More

To the men, who sit when worship begins.
Women frozen forcing a grin.
Clap, shout, and dance with glee if the music is about
anything ordinary.
When it comes to our Lord let a peep not be heard.
We must sit still and be reserved.
Savior, the Lamb that's not who I am.
I want to praise with every ounce that I can.
Sound the trumpet.
Pluck a string.
Did I hear a drum?
Let's sing.
Shout to the King!
Hosanna, Hosanna!
You've risen it's true.
Clap with joy, let us all praise you.

Spring Like Confetti

Thankfulness spilling fully from me.
Springing like confetti for all to see.
Blessings bestowed.
For all to behold.
Pouring down like rain.
I soak it up as it drenches out the pain.
Lord you give so abundantly.
I want thankfulness to constantly, spring like confetti.

I'm Free

Hallelujah, I'm free!
You've extended grace and mercy.
Heavy chains wore me down.
Jesus, you tossed them to the ground.
Hallelujah, I'm free!
You've extended grace and mercy.
Cloaked in your name.
Yeshua, you bare all my shame.
Hallelujah, I'm free!
You've extended grace and mercy.
All hail to our King.
Your praises I sing.
Hallelujah, I'm free!

Made in the USA
Middletown, DE
14 November 2018